# Bellarina

ISBN 979-8-88540-772-4 (paperback)
ISBN 979-8-88540-773-1 (digital)



Christian Faith Publishing
832 Park Avenue
Meadville, PA 16335
www.christianfaithpublishing.com

Printed in the United States of America

# Bellarina

Pamela Blume

Magic dust, fairy wings, flying high in the sky! These are a few of Bellarina's favorite things. Bellarina, a sixteen-year-old fairy, is taking a trip to Fairy Mountain that she has so patiently awaited since she first heard of the mountain when she was just a young fairy.

Fairy Mountain is where the young fairies go for a vacation before they begin their careers at home. B, as her close friends and family call her, is eager to finally explore the wondrous things found there, such as the rivers as pink as bubble gum, the trees as tall as skyscrapers, and the softest grass like a puppy's fur. She is thrilled to show off her new rainbow fairy wings that match her beautiful makeup and her brightly colored clothes that she received for her new voyage! Most of all, B is anticipating the number of new friends she will make because of her kind heart and sweet spirit. She is known for being full of love.

Once B arrives at Fairy Mountain, she is captivated by the beautiful scenery and pleasant aroma of vanilla wafting through the air. As expected, B is quickly known as the kindest fairy that any of the other fairies have ever encountered. They flutter about, speaking of her cheer that she spreads to all.

This rumor of a kind visitor has begun to upset the princess of the mountain, Faylah. Faylah is always stressed, and she is never happy.

While on her vacation, B has met multiple fairy families and helped them with their children when needed, helped the elderly fairies with their cleaning, and even spent time with the fairies who are new to the mountain. B chooses kindness toward others, and this kindness can sometimes make one tiresome.

Tired yet full of happiness, B flutters off to her vacation house, so amazed at all the colorful houses and rivers. She is taking in the soft, sweet vanilla scent, when all of a sudden…the amazement is abruptly ended by tall, dark fairy guards who arrive to B's surprise.

"Ma'am, you must stop being nice to all you see, or else you will be doomed to a lifetime of darkness by our princess, Faylah!" they shout.

"Oh no!" cries B. *What must I do to survive and not live a life that is full of doom and darkness?* B thinks. "I cannot be mean to anyone," she continues. "Wait, what did I even do? How is being too nice a crime?" B asks the guards.

"Faylah disapproves of your nosiness on the mountain. You must leave at once!" the dark fairy guards demand.

Alone and afraid, B swirls through the sky as fast as lightning. Without warning, a vicious storm begins to bring about danger over Fairy Mountain. The rain is like a train with its violent force. B is in confusion as she searches for shelter. There is none to be found. All the fairies in Fairy Mountain are too timid to help B for fear of their own lives.

Looking and searching for shelter, B finds a mysterious cave on the side of Fairy Mountain. The cave is hidden by the skyscraper trees and stunning blue roses. Safe until the storm passes, B takes a brief sigh of relief.

Still hungry and scared, she is thinking of her next move and how this trip has just become her worst endeavor yet, when she hears the soft scratch of nails on the interior of the cave. Through the roses, a dim light appears to reveal the face of Faylah! Faylah knew that this would be the only shelter B could find from the ferocious storm.

9

Without hesitation, Faylah attacks B in a fit of rage! Faylah uses her evil to try and hurt B, but B is only retaliating for her own safety. As Faylah continues to terrorize her opponent, B parries the blows.

Finally, B screams out, "Stop! I cannot fight you! I know that you dislike me, but I am only trying to be kind. Please leave me alone and let me leave peacefully."

Faylah, tired and confused, replies with "Why are you so nice? Why do you care about other fairies and their feelings anyways?"

"I care because I know that everyone has their own story to tell. Everyone is unique and their stories matter. We can all help one another. Can we please try to talk about our differences and see what the true problem is?" asks B.

"I guess," sighs Faylah.

"Well, you're a princess. What do you even have to be angry with?" B asks Faylah.

"If you must know, I am angry that everyone thinks I must act perfectly and must always make the right decisions! Don't they know I am imperfect and that I am only just now learning how to take over Fairy Mountain and rule as queen one day? If I make the wrong decision, so many fairies will be displeased. I am so unhappy."

"Oh, Faylah," replies B with a sense of empathy. "I am so sorry that you have that amount of pressure on you. No one expects you to be perfect. I have been so excited to come to Fairy Mountain for years because of the exciting things I hear about the community here. You must be doing something right."

"Yeah, like what?" asks Faylah.

"I know that all of the fairy homes are well taken care of and that the land is magnificently beautiful," says B.

"It's because I work endlessly! I have no time off to do what I want to do," states Faylah.

"Well, maybe it is time for you to hire some helpers to help with the community," replies B. "I have learned that working together can help remove a lot of stress while actually gaining new friends! We are all different, and with our strengths we help each other to grow into the best us we can be. Sometimes it just takes trust and a little courage to try."

"Well, may—maybe I could," Faylah says, hesitating. "Could you help me with this project, B?"

"Why, yes, of course!" shouts B. "I would be happy to! When do we start?"

"Um, maybe after this horrible storm," Faylah says with a laugh.

"Sounds like a plan," responds B.

From then on, the fairy princess of Fairy Mountain has a changed heart.

She is no longer mean to others. She shares her duties among the community, and she sees what her fellow villagers are capable of doing together. This makes Fairy Mountain even more enticing for visitors, and it helps relax the princess. Faylah and B are now the closest of friends. Even though Bellarina returned home, she still visits Fairy Mountain to check in with her new best friend, Faylah, very frequently.

The End

# About the Author

Pamela Blume is currently a fourth-grade English Language Arts teacher living in North Carolina with her loving husband, two amazing teenagers, and their crazy German Shepherd. She has been teaching for nine years, but she has always wanted to be an author. Pamela feels that writing is a work of art that produces material able to be appreciated by everyone at any age level. God has blessed her with this opportunity to be able to produce a children's book at this time in life that she wants to share with others. Pamela Blume hopes you enjoy her work!